Illustrated by

Samantha A. Stoker

Prepared for publication by

Ryan D. Stoker

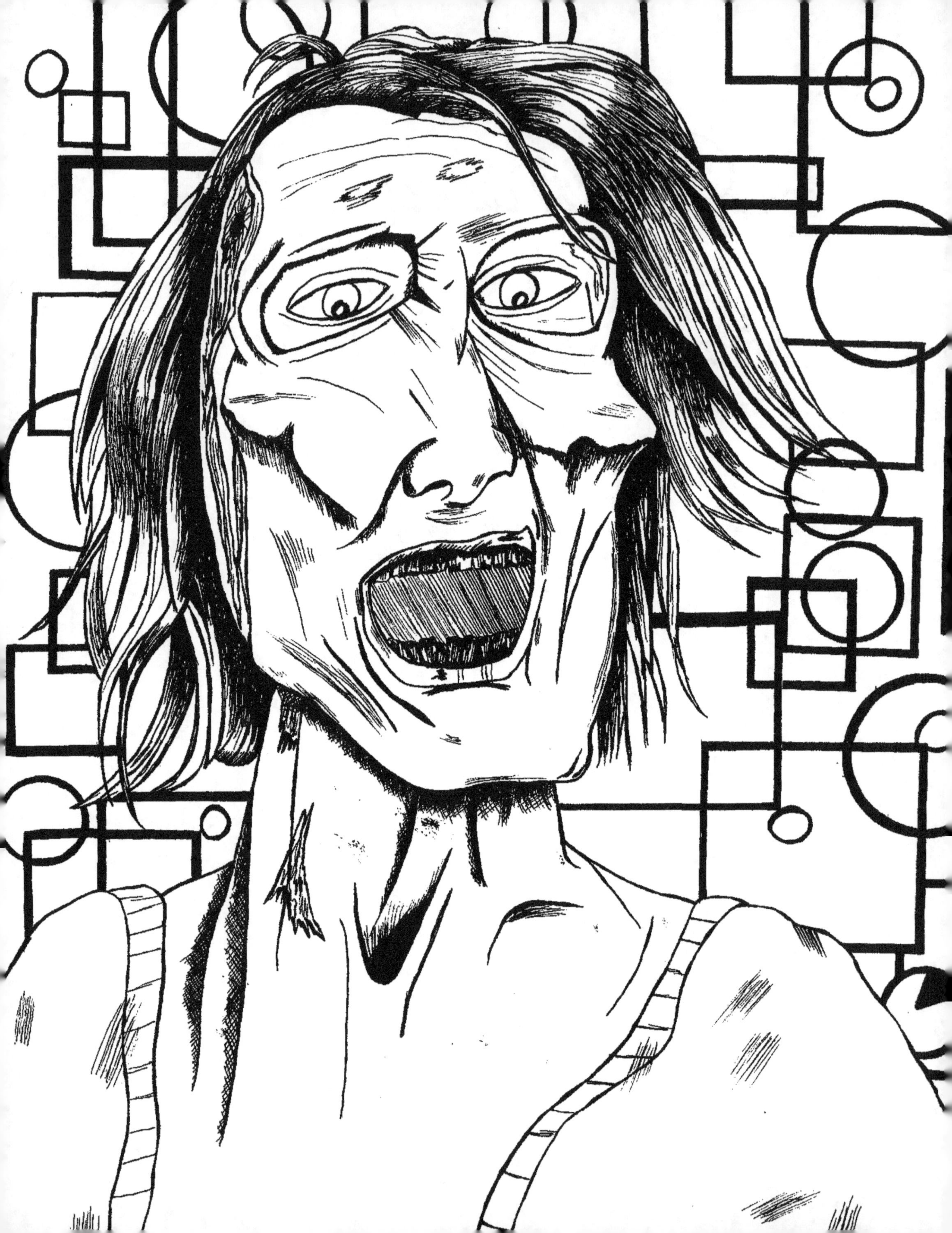

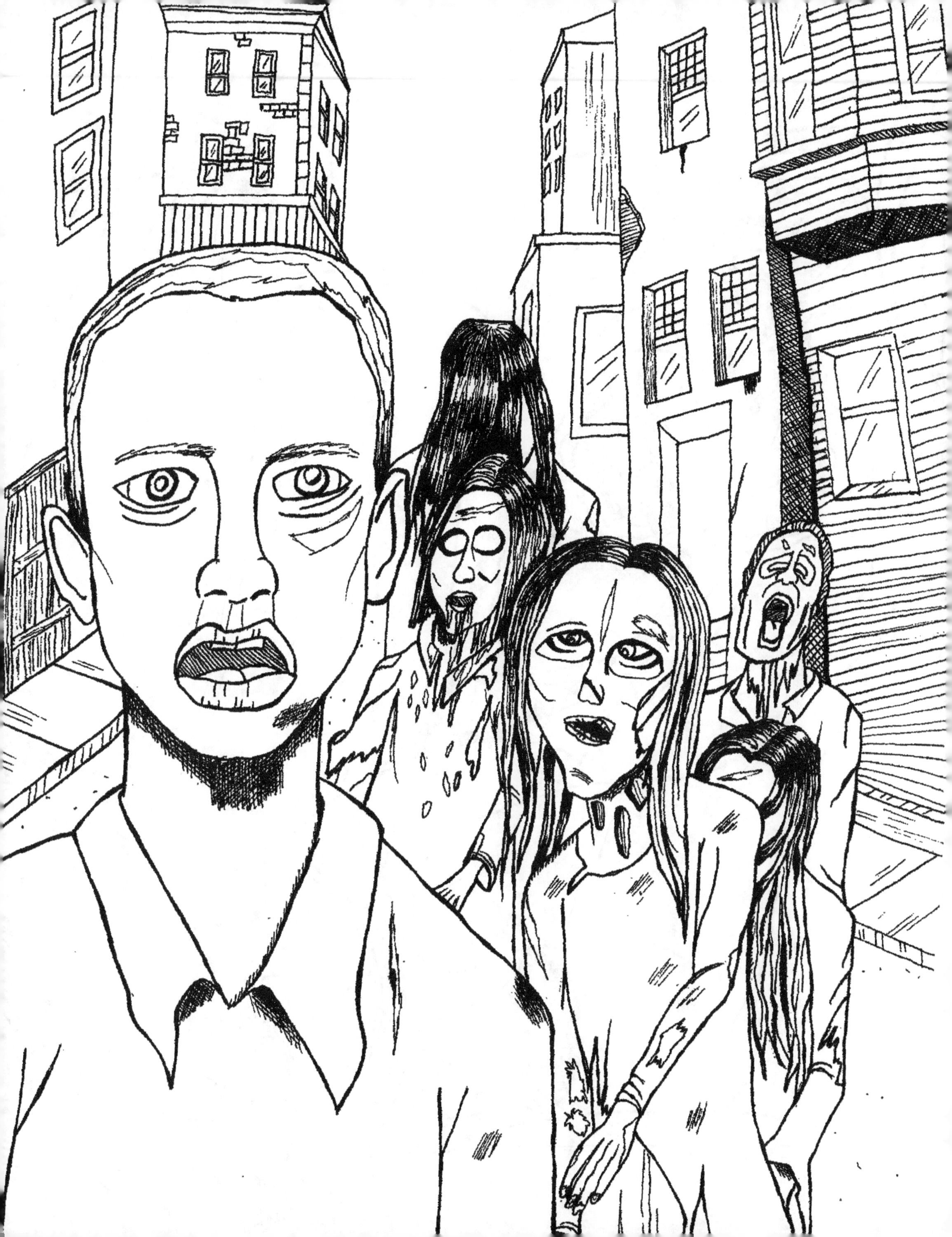

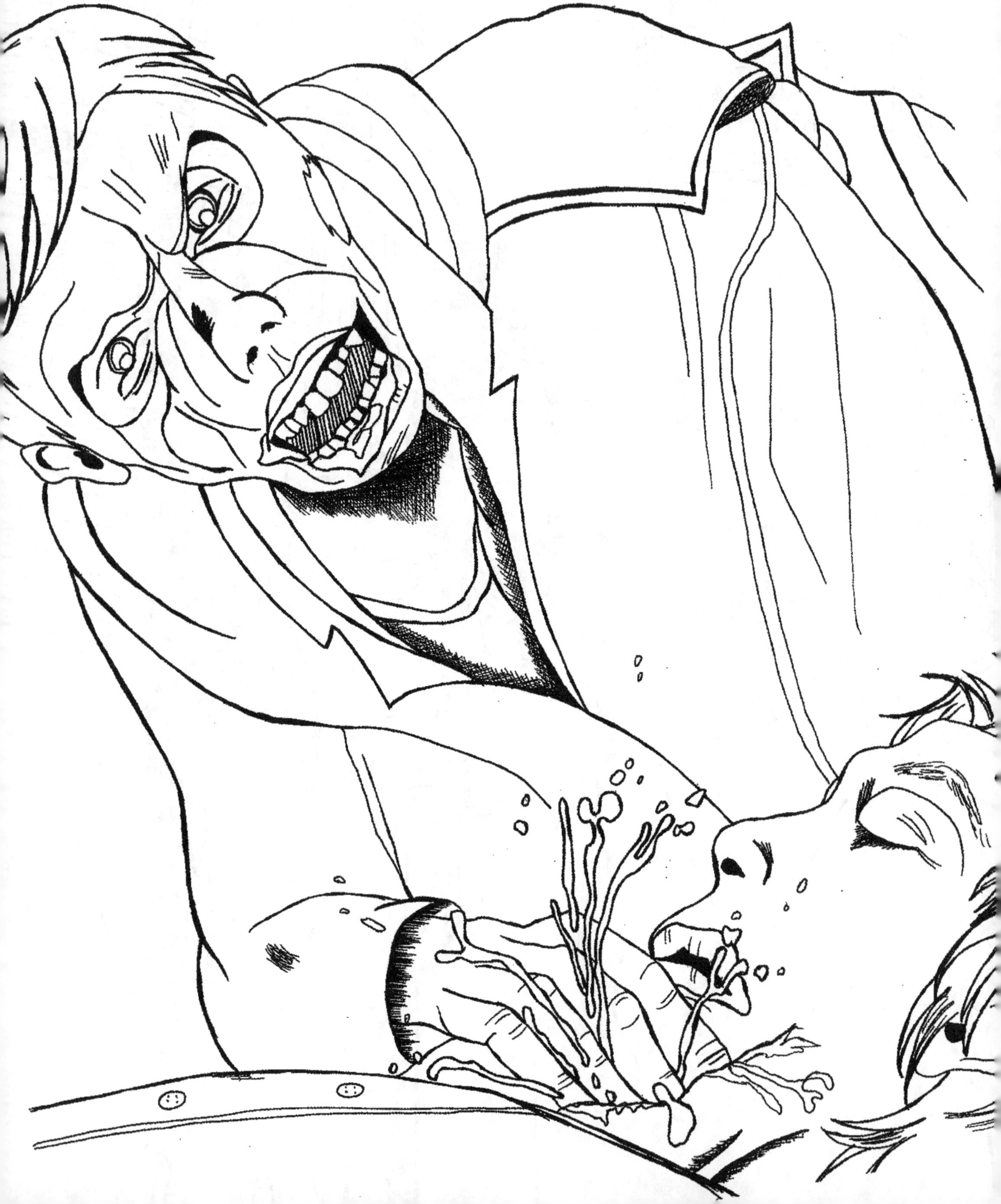

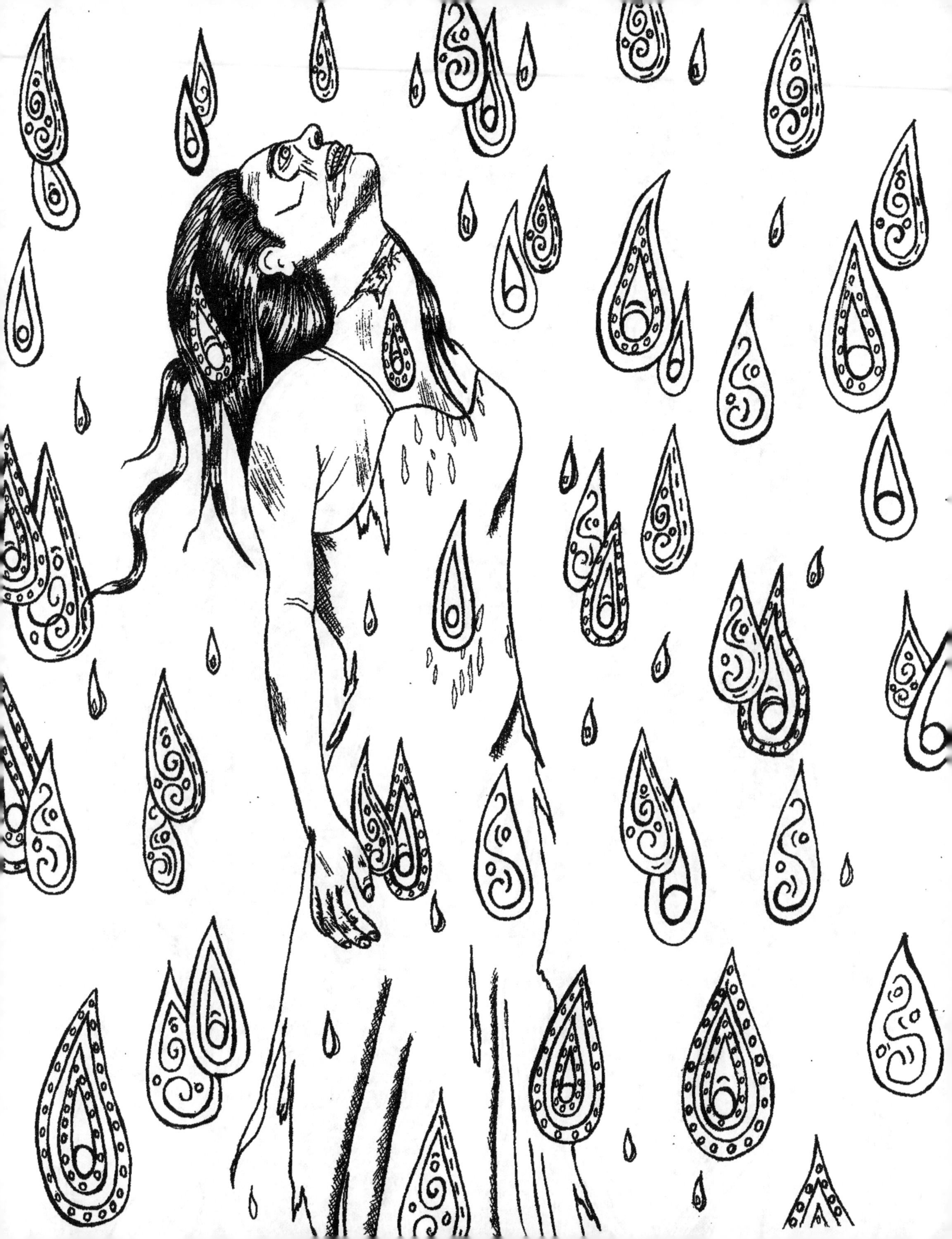

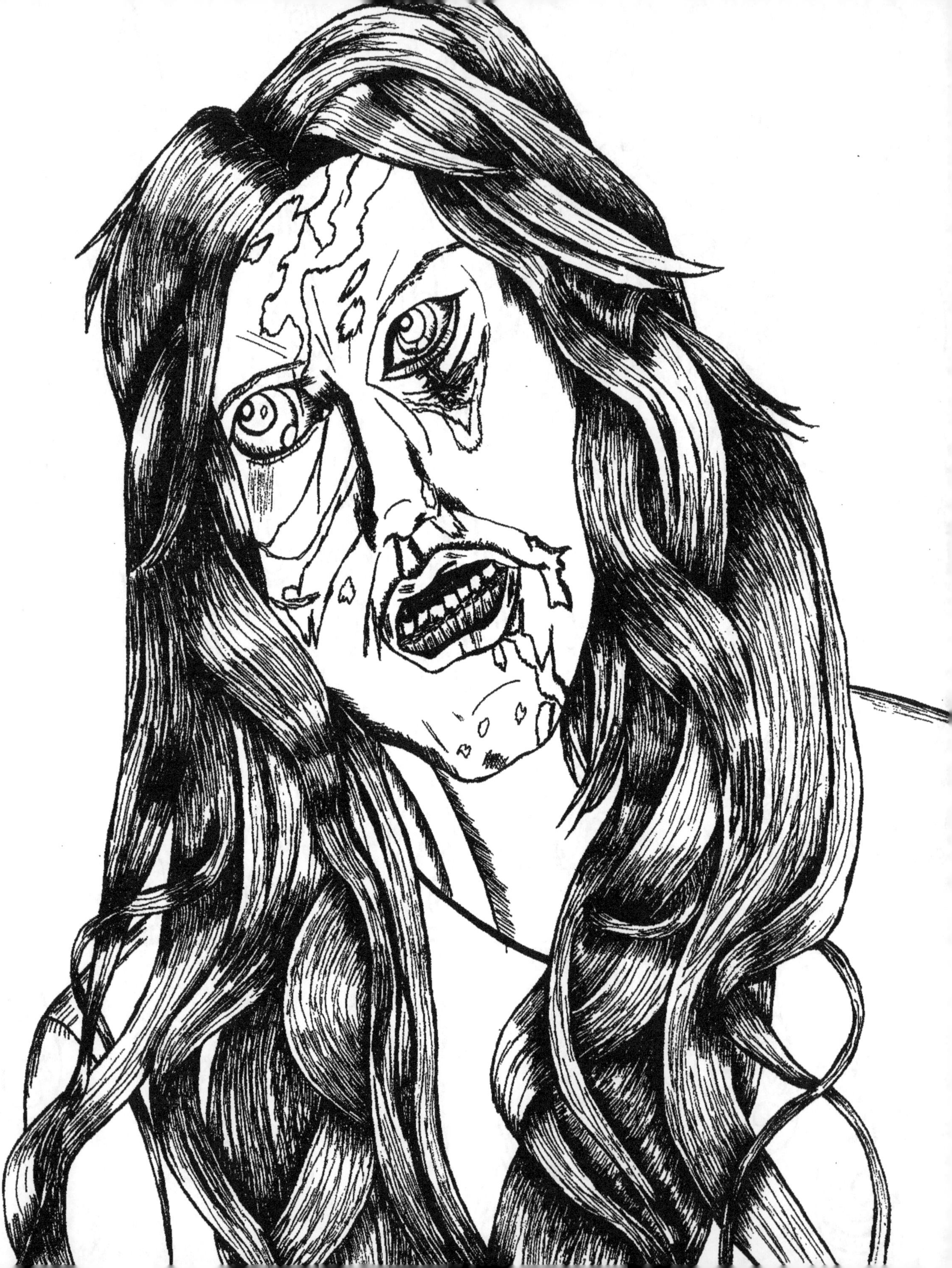

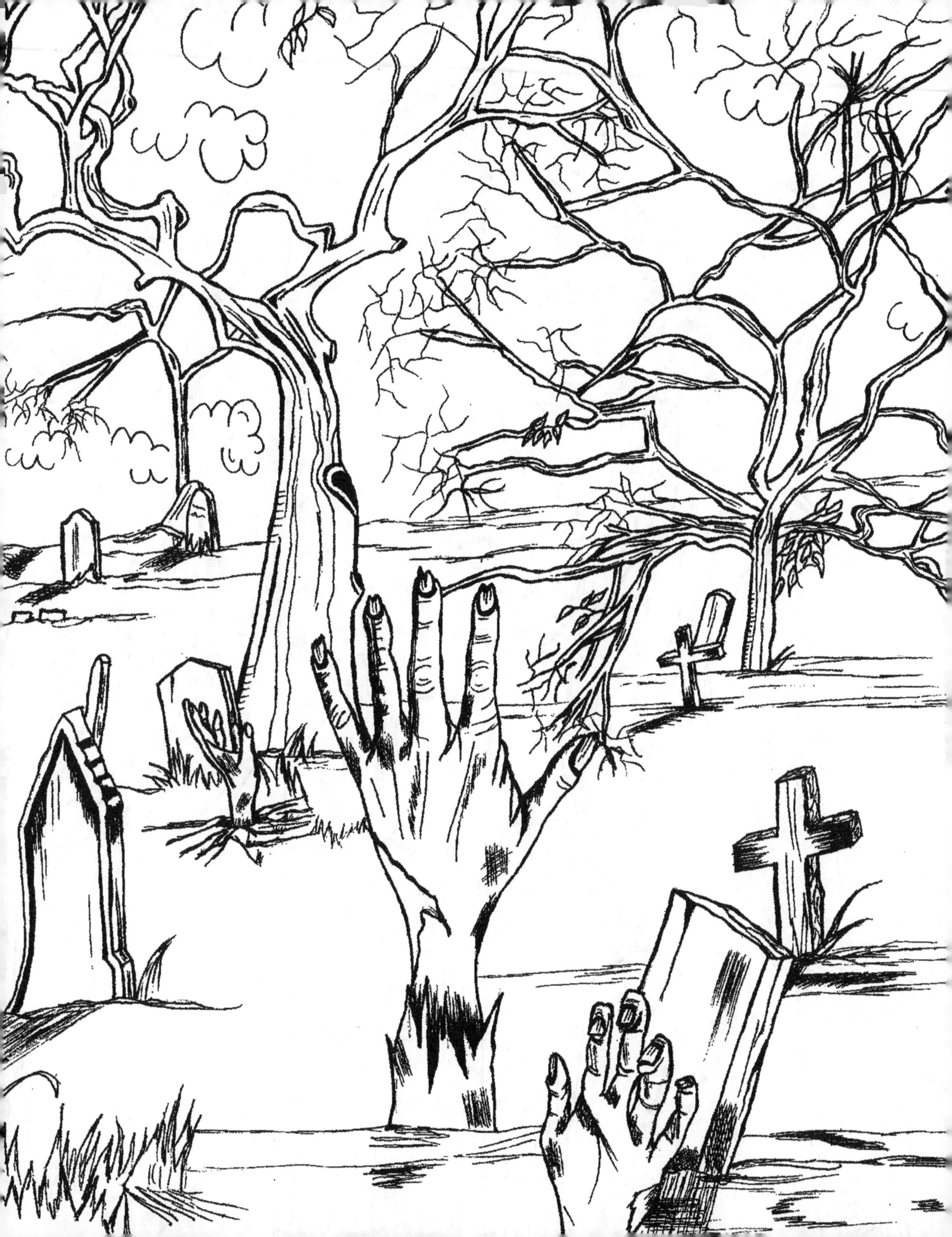

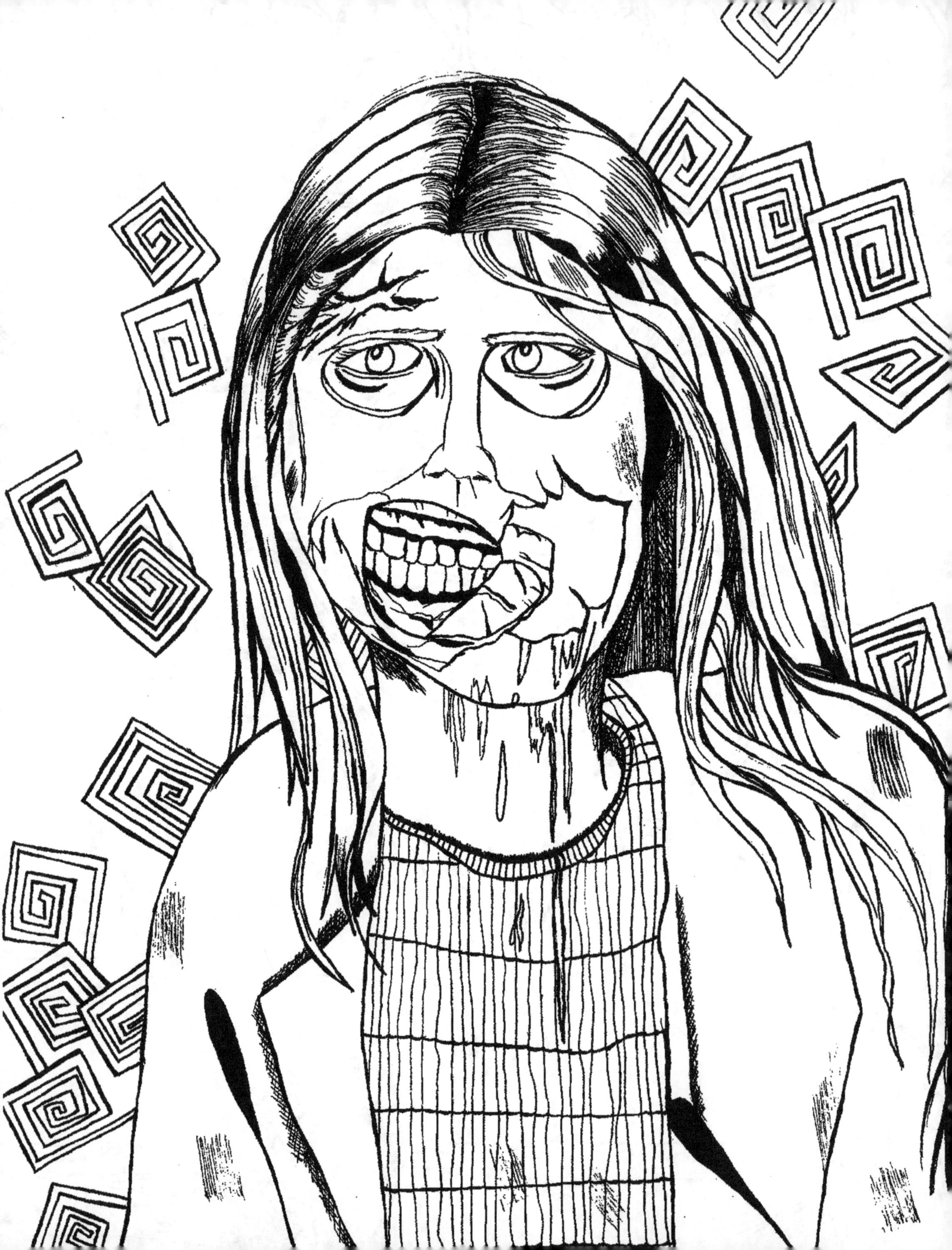

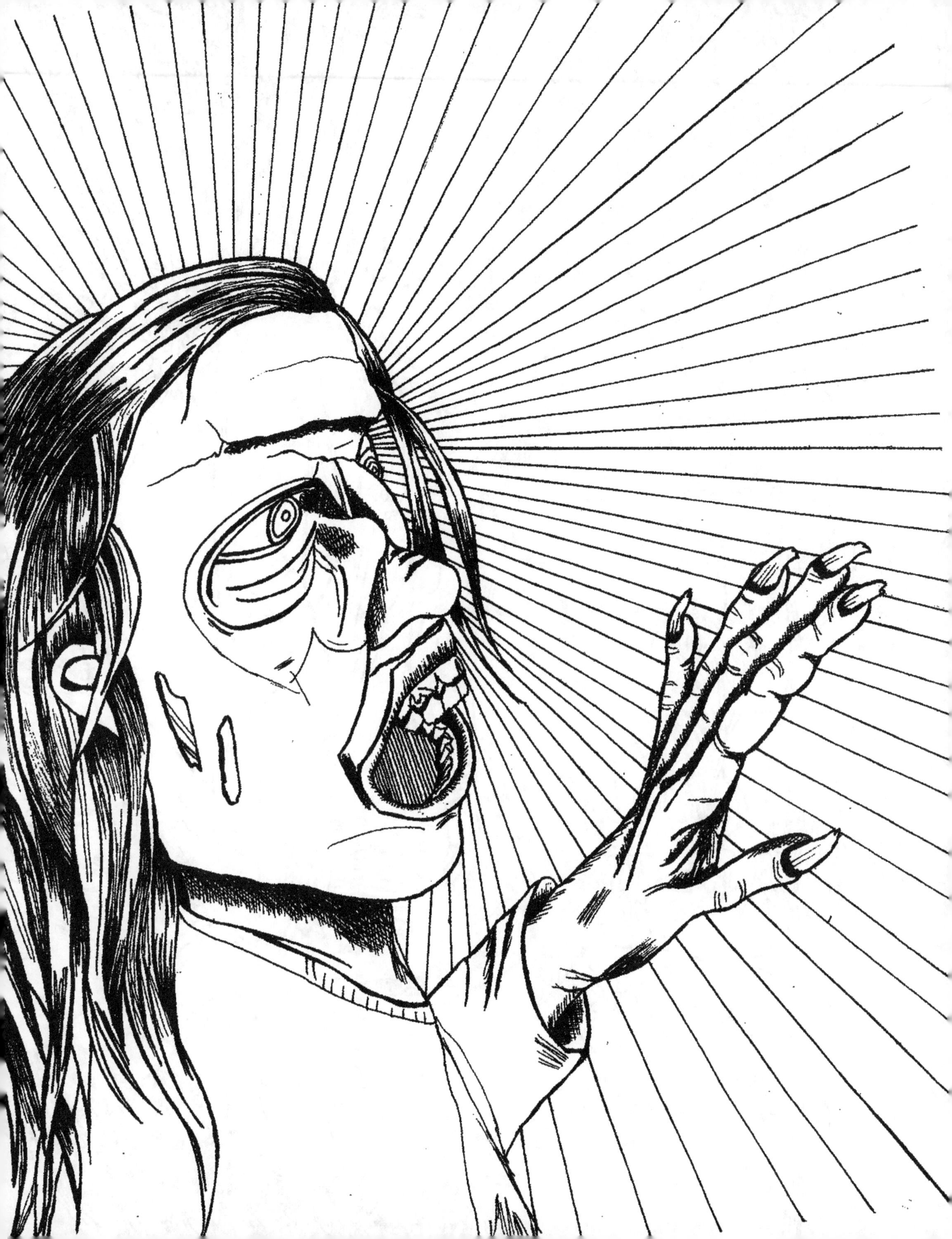

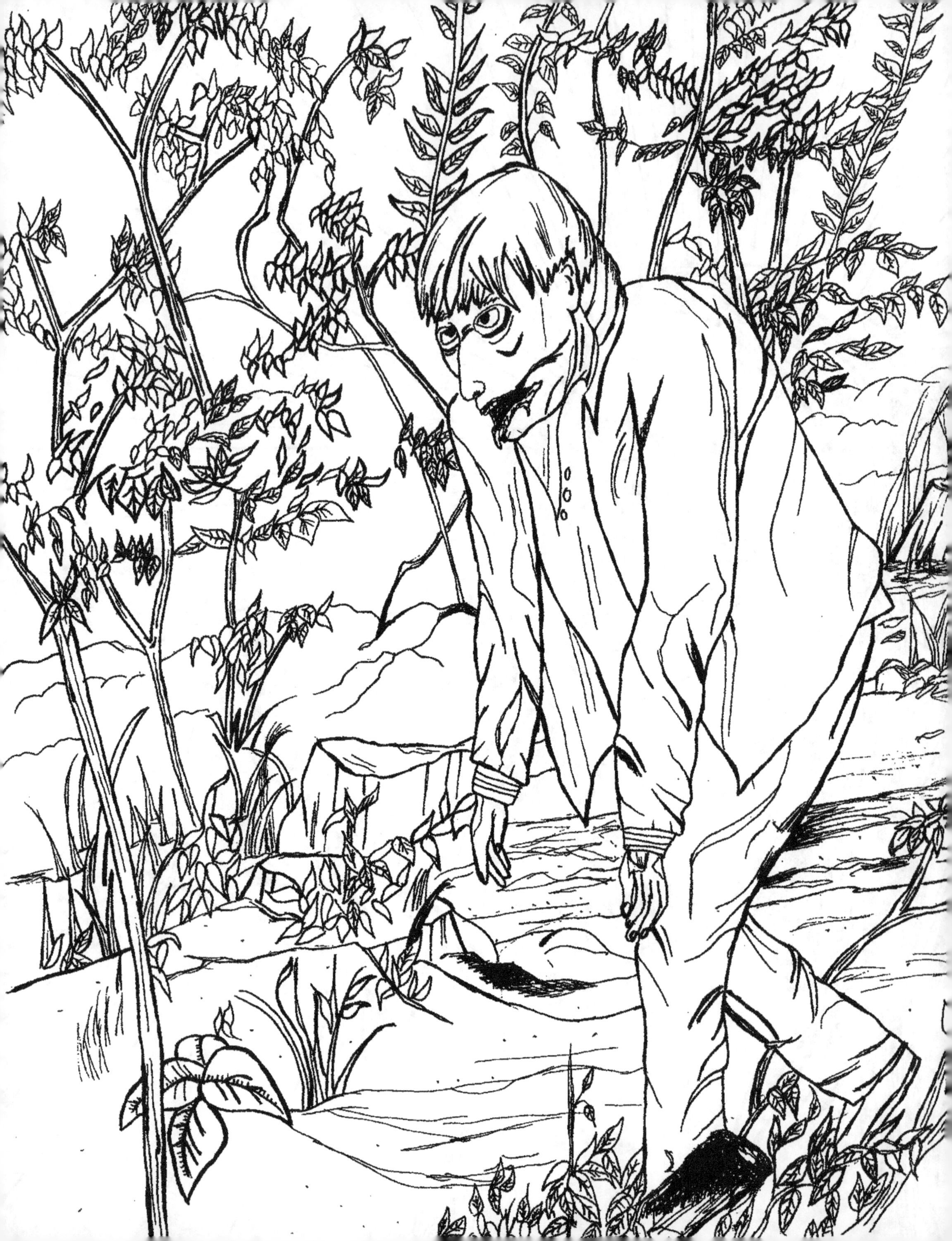

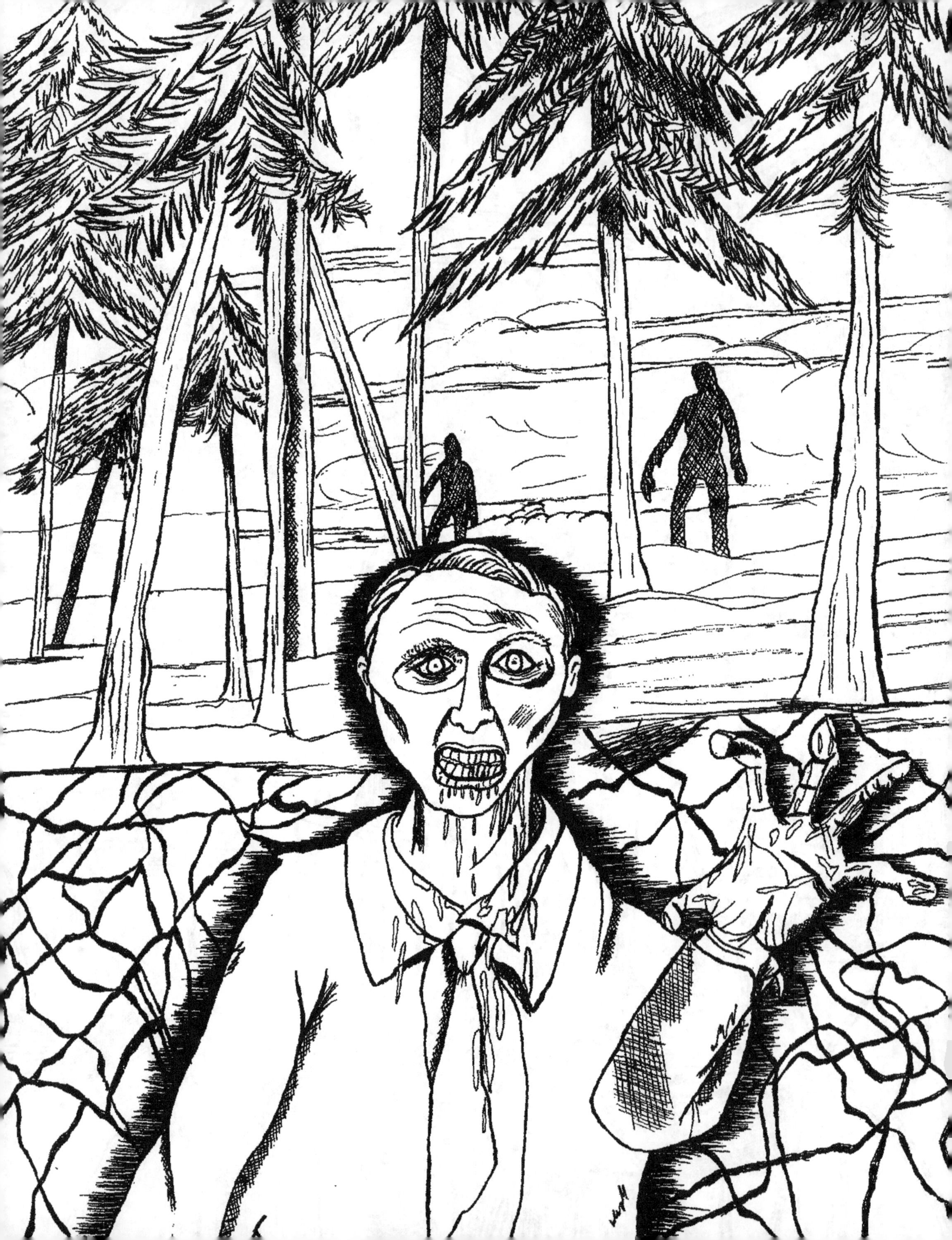

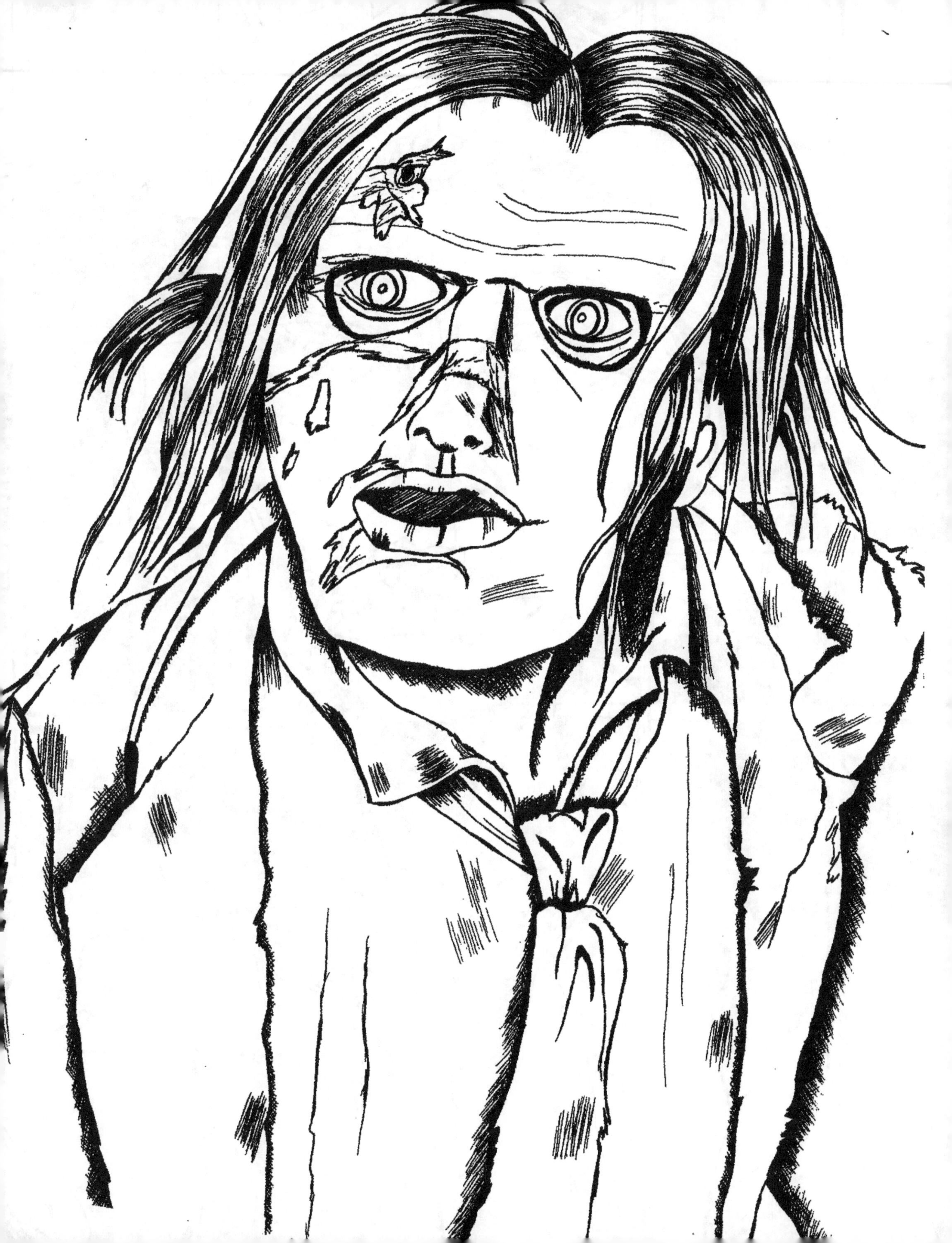

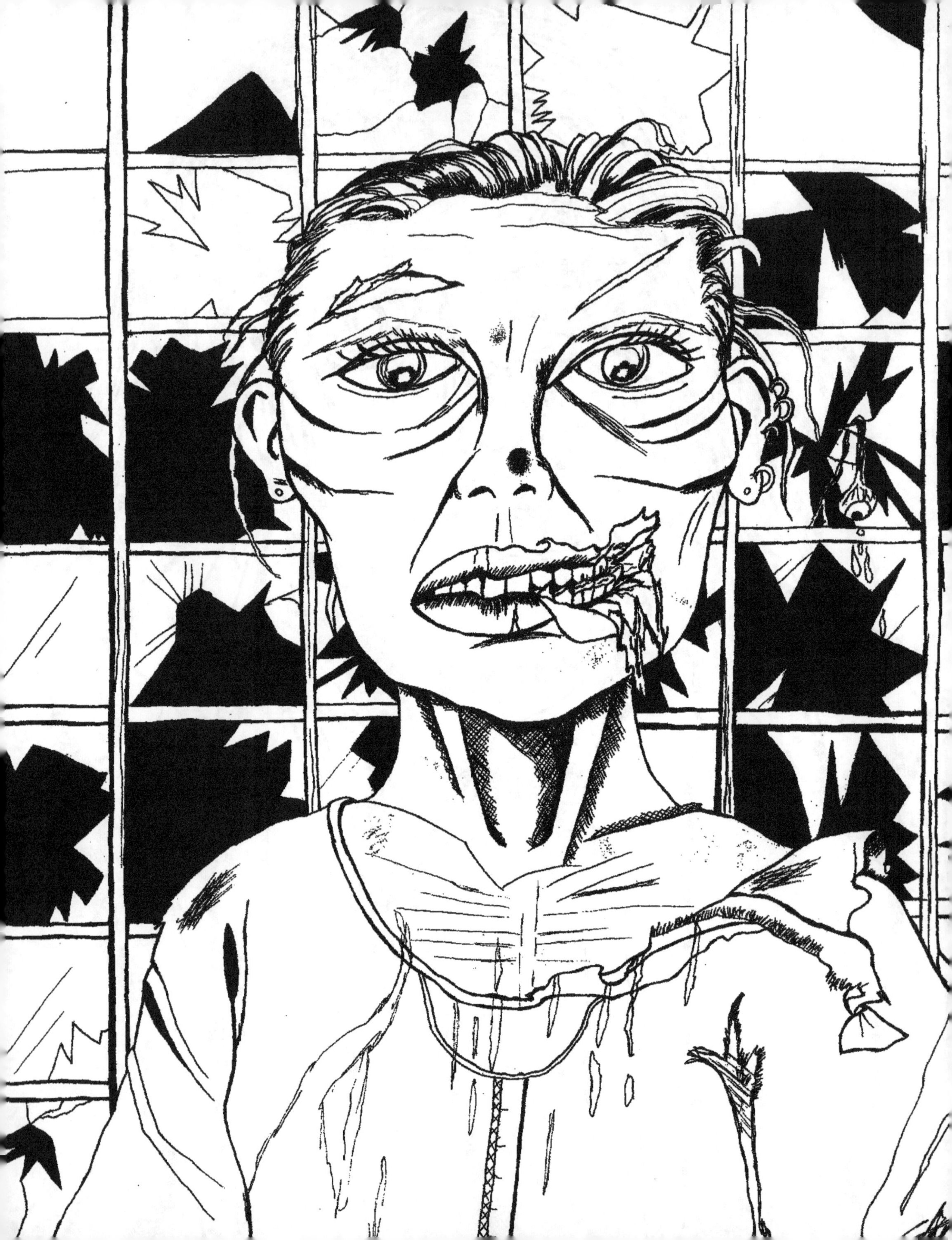

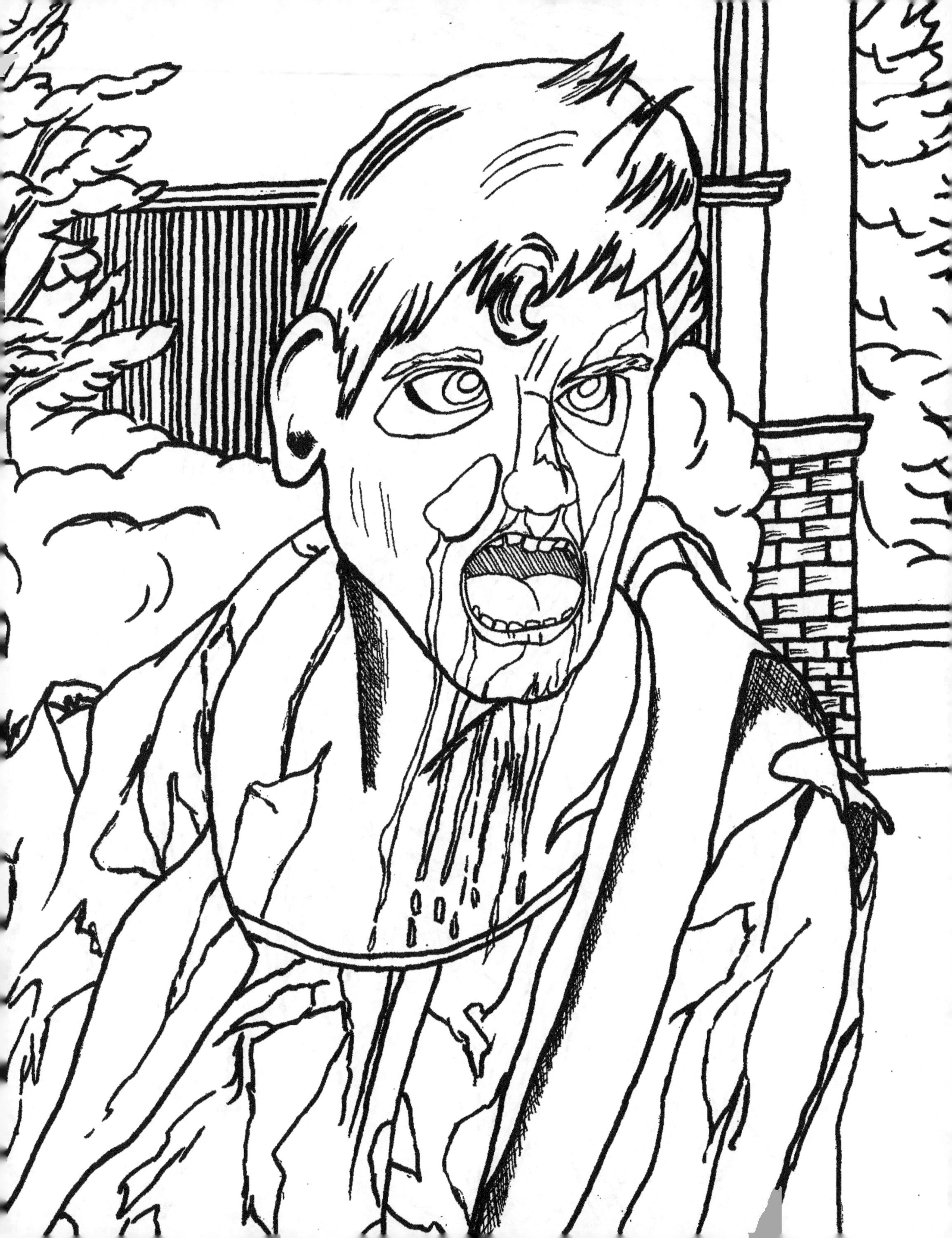

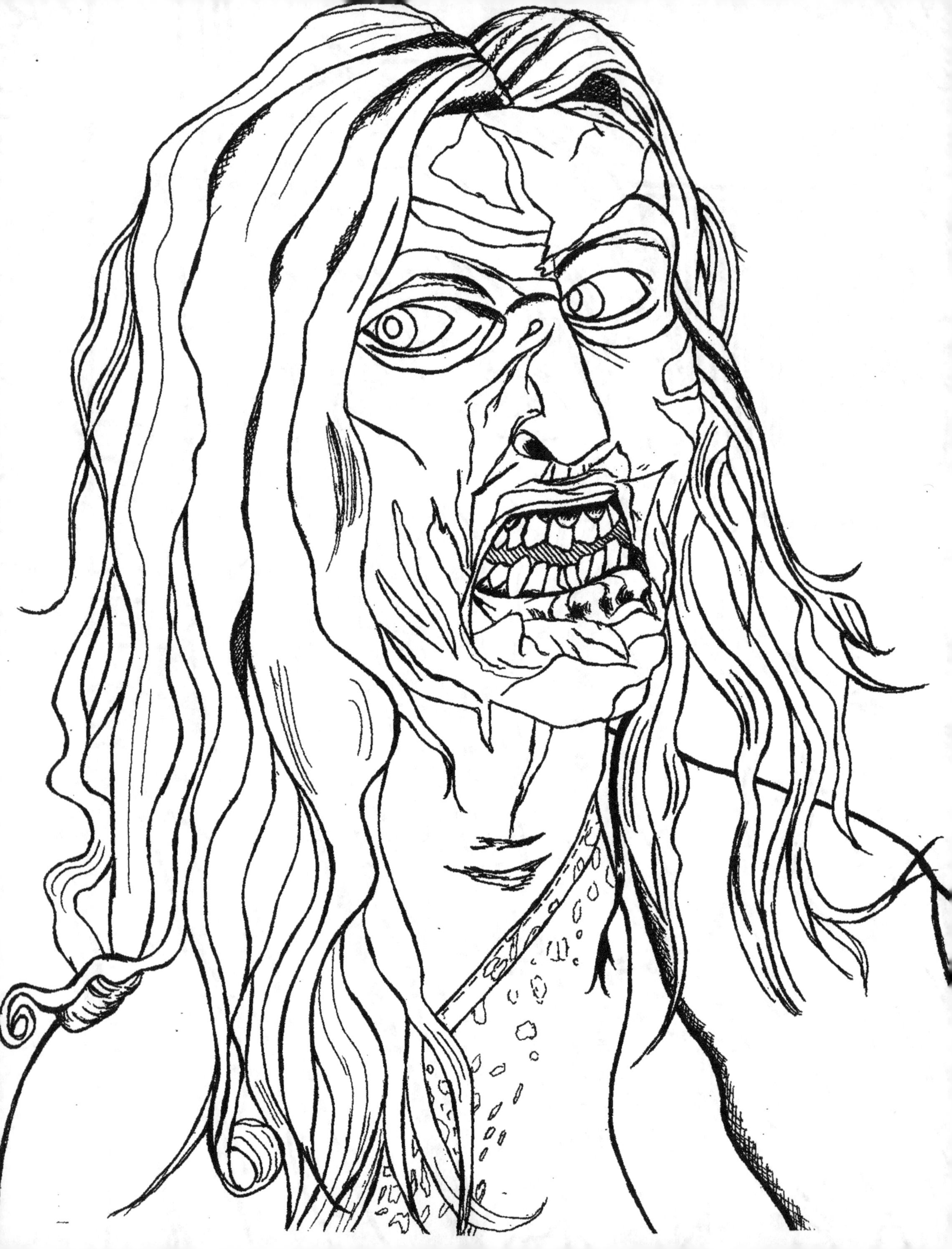

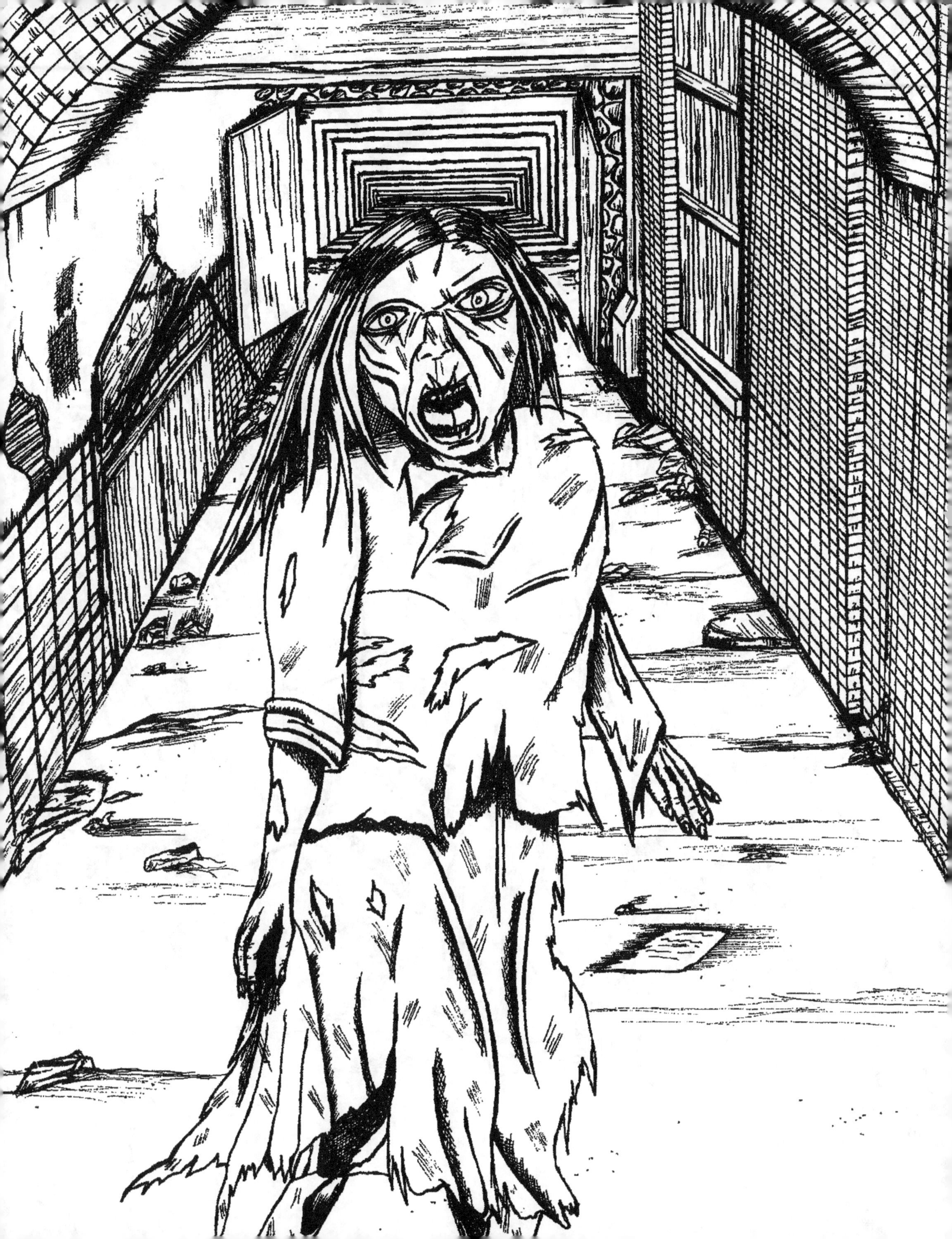

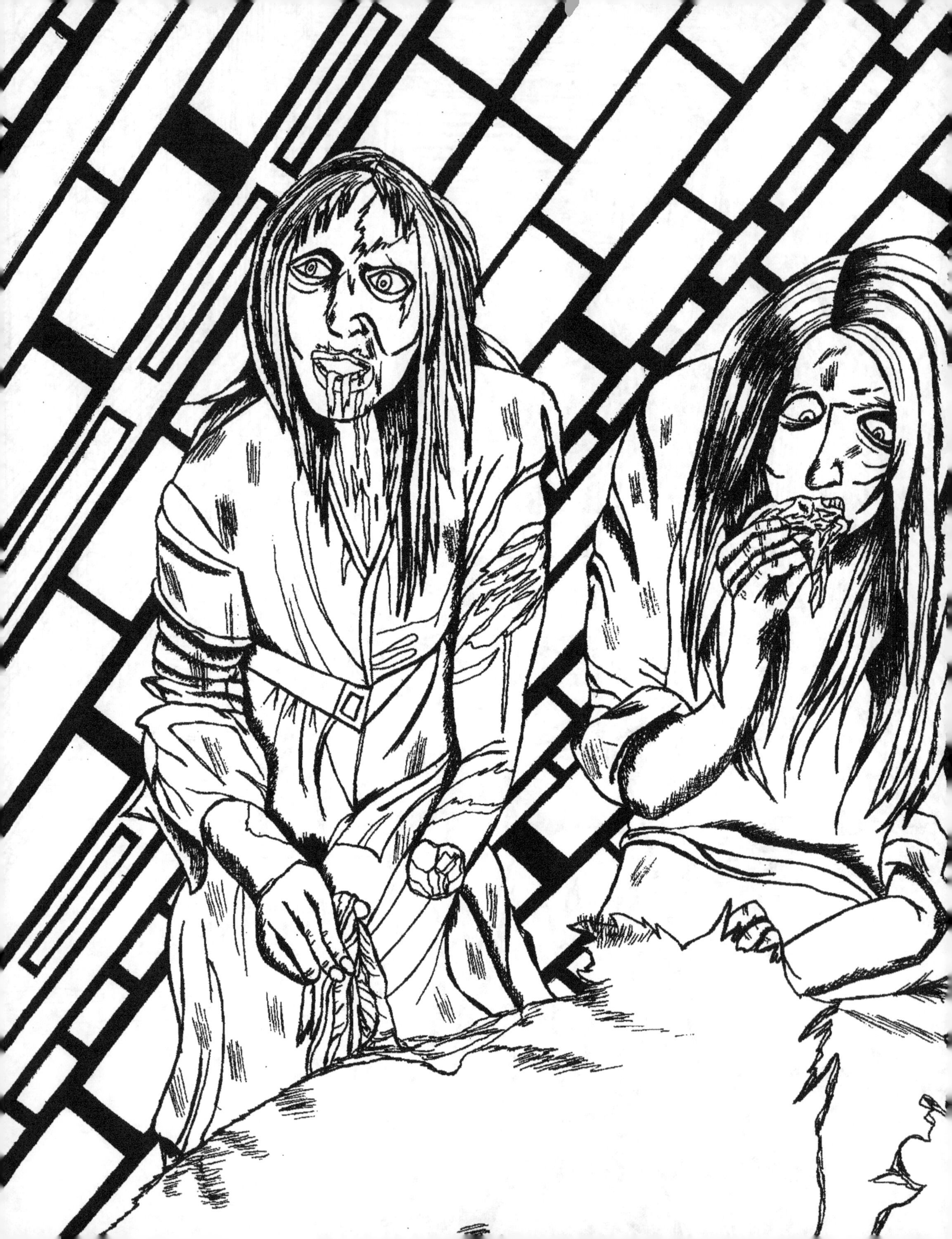

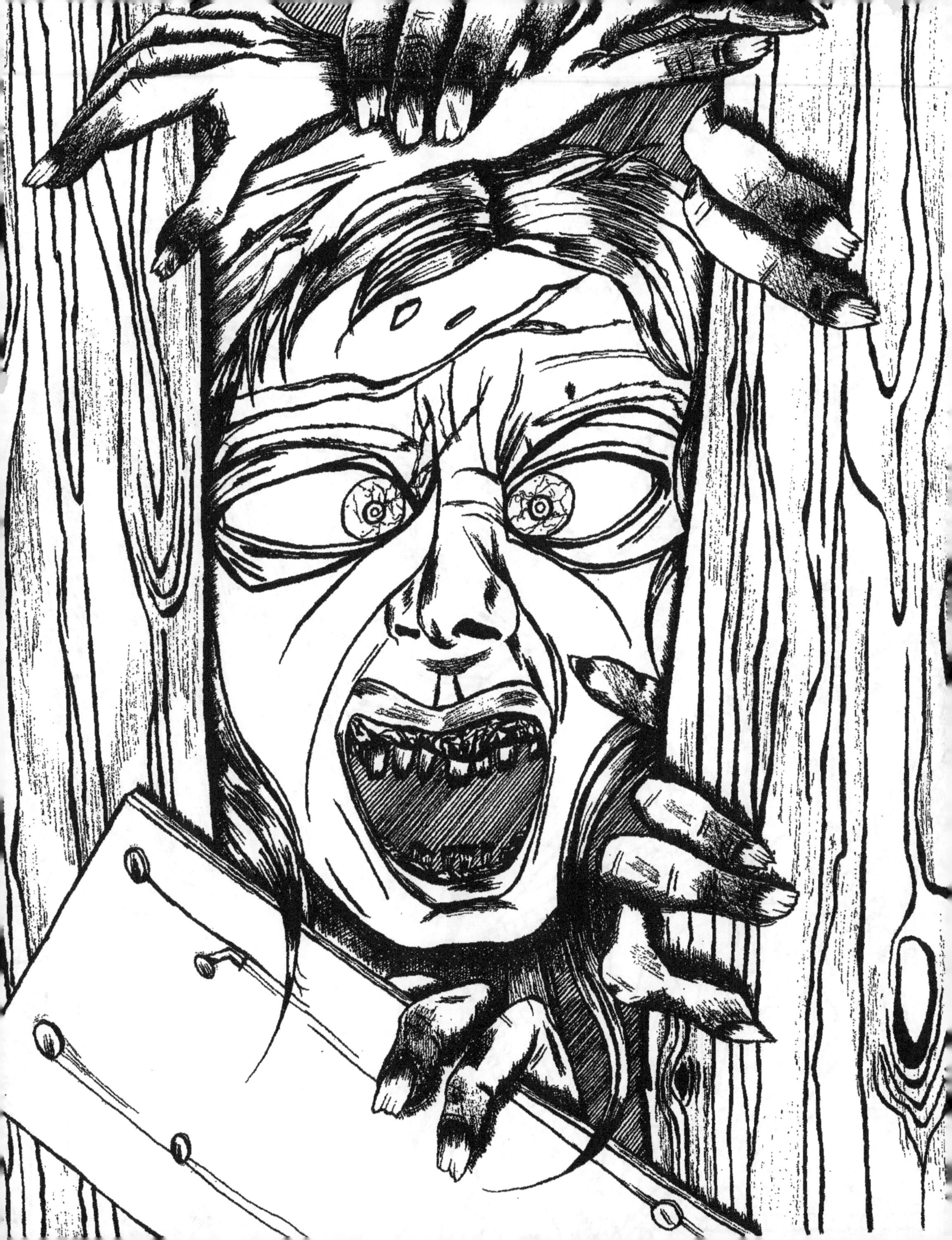

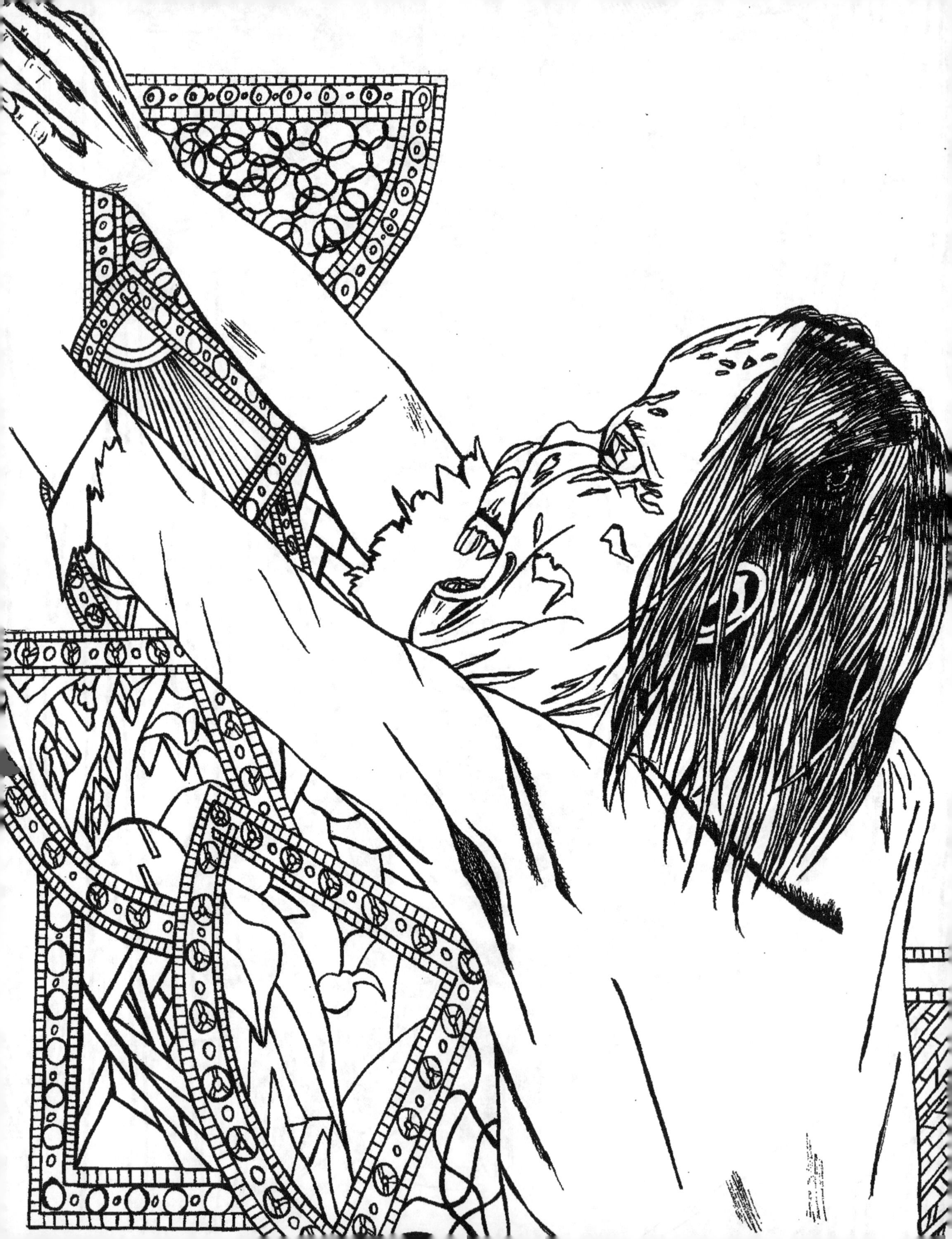

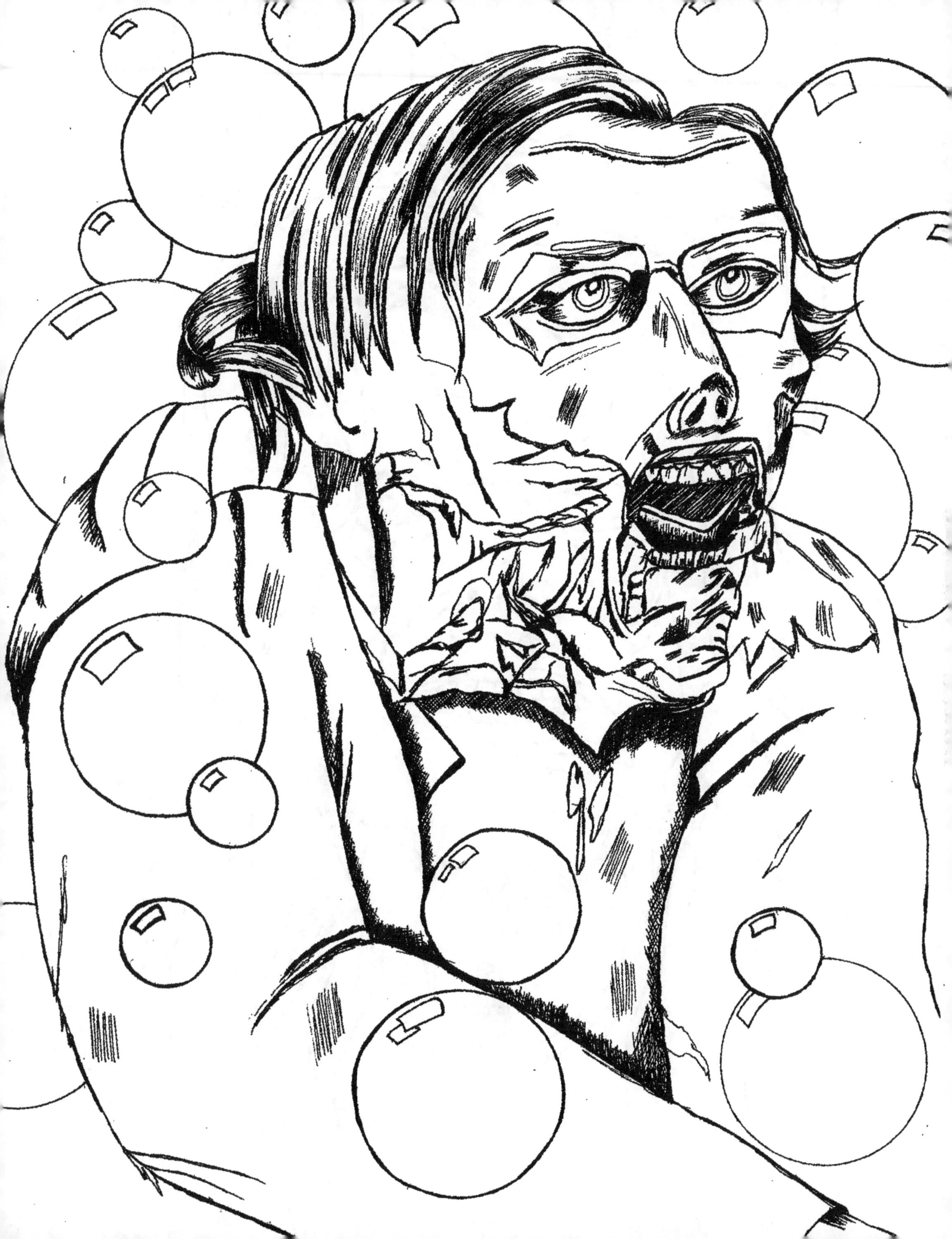

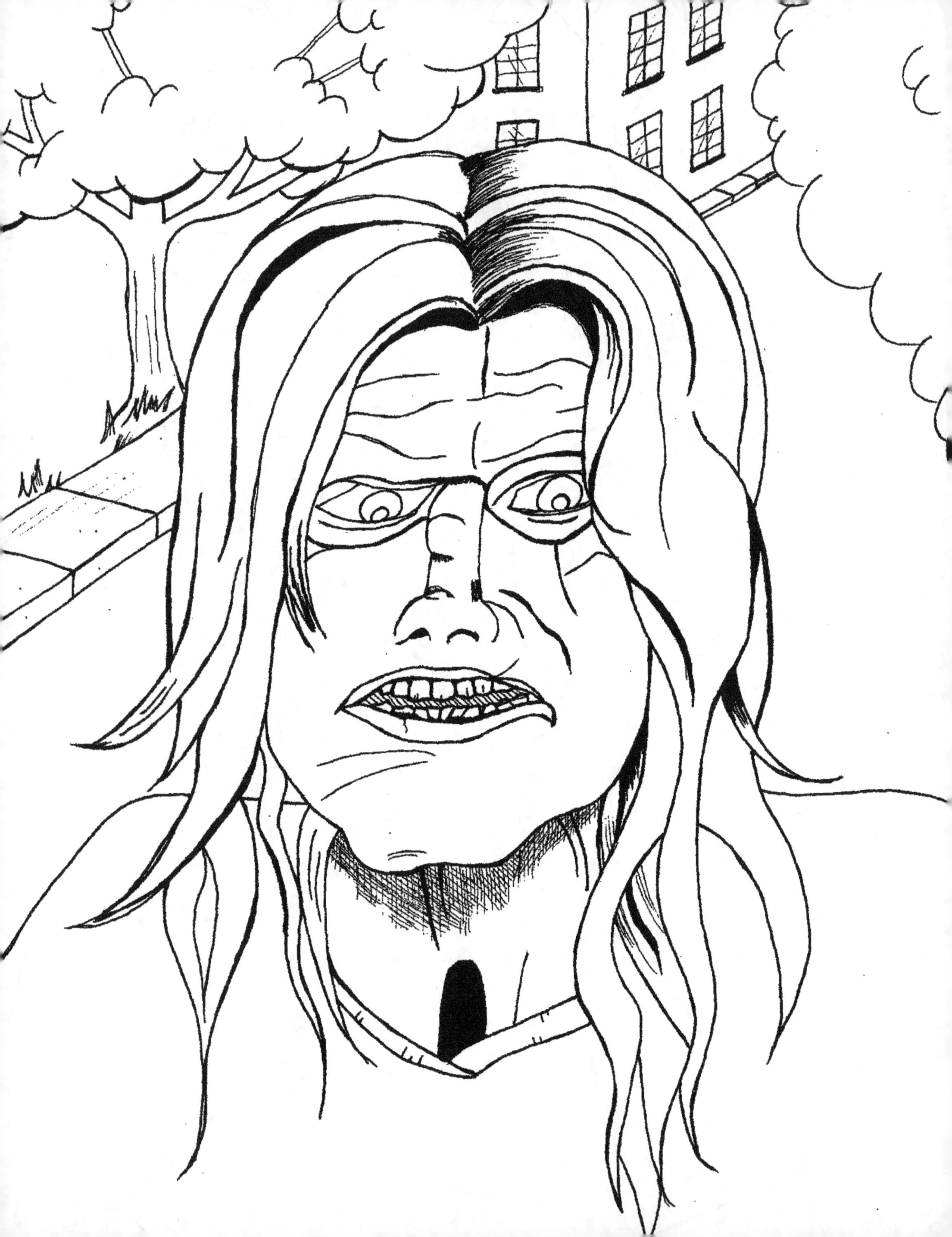

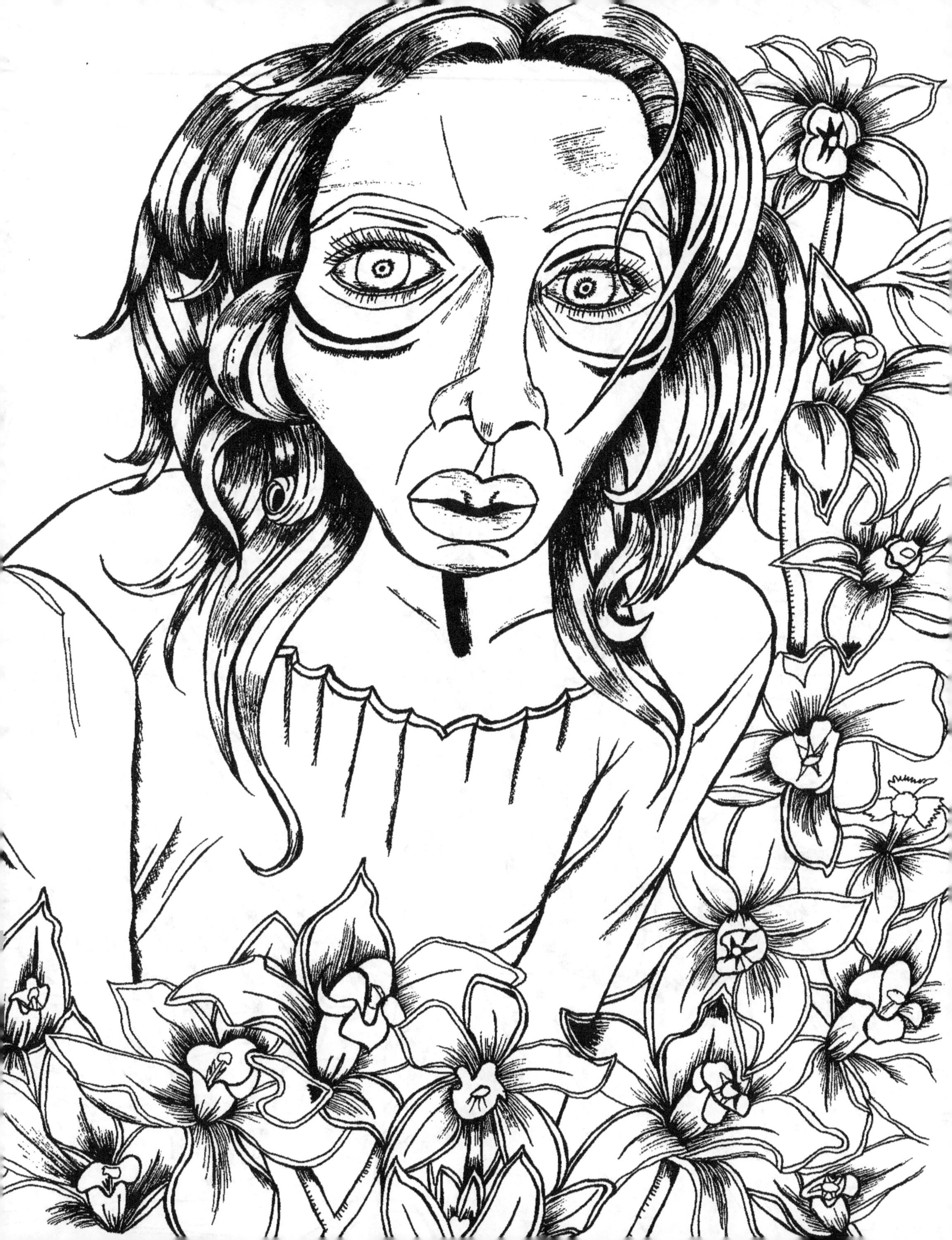

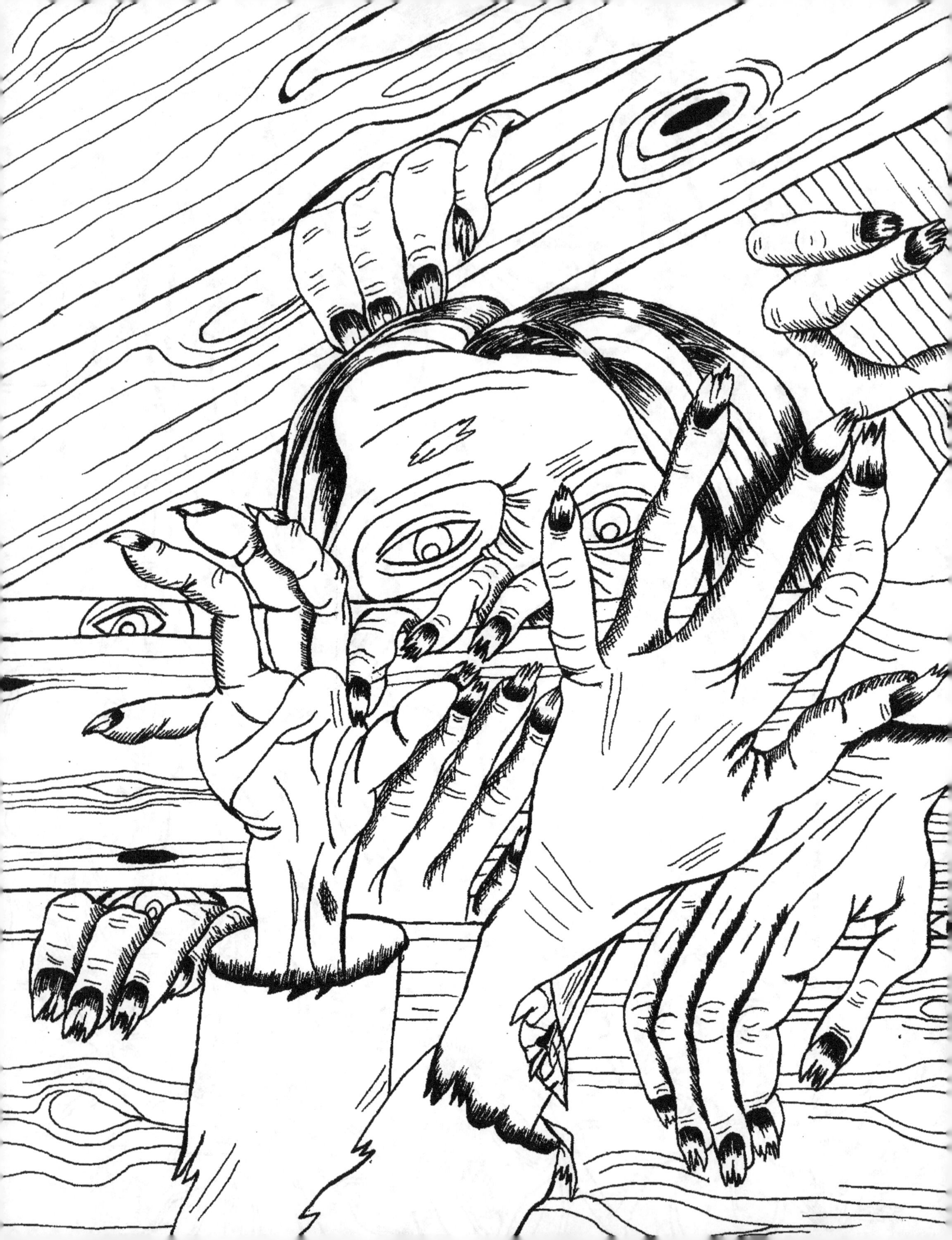

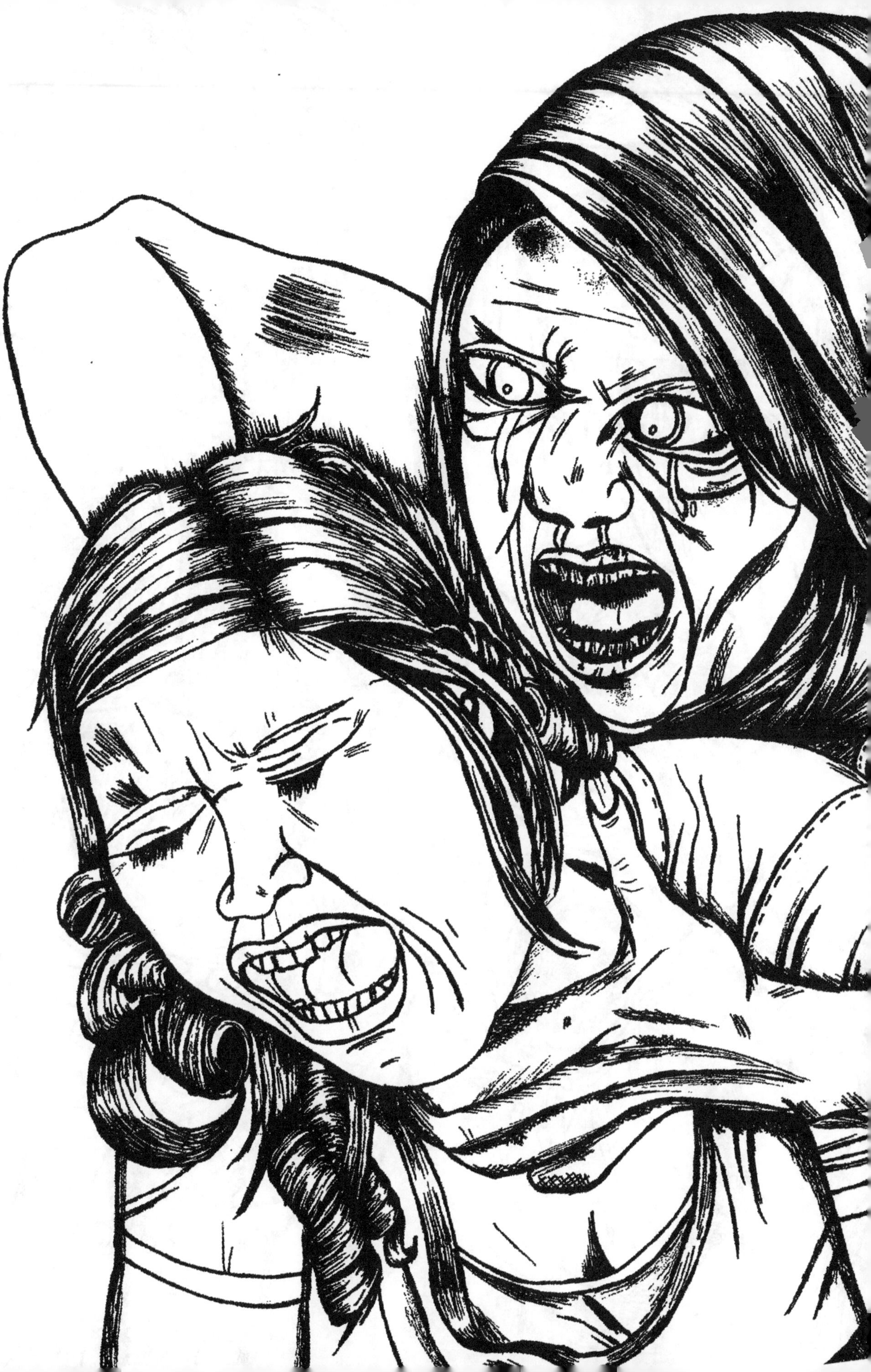

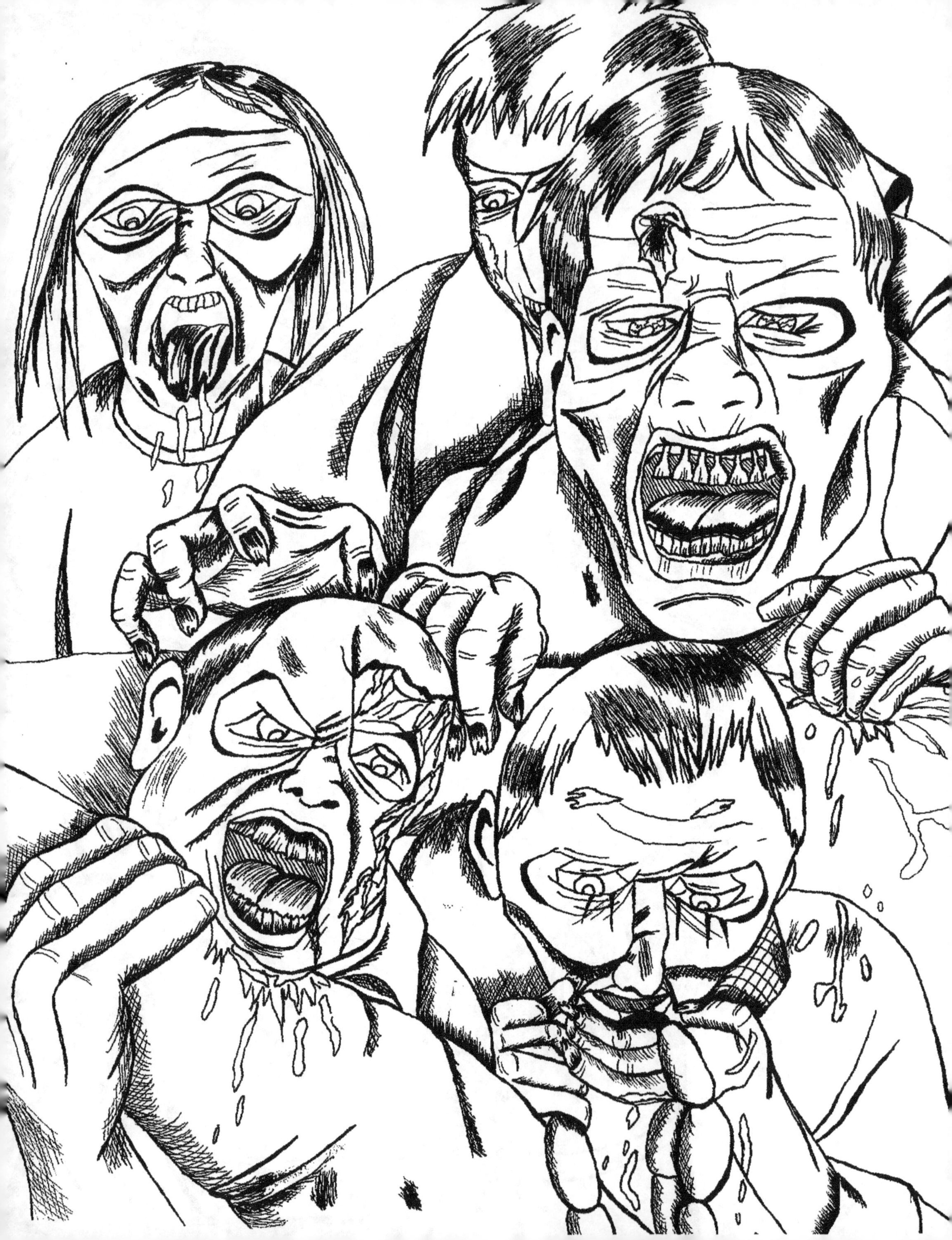

www.ingramcontent.com/pod-product-compliance
Lightning Source LLC
Chambersburg PA
CBHW080532190526
45169CB00008B/3137
* 9 7 8 1 5 2 3 9 6 3 9 3 5 *